Some Moments in a Gentle War

poems by

David MacRae Landon

Finishing Line Press
Georgetown, Kentucky

Some Moments in a Gentle War

ACKNOWLEDGMENTS

Birmingham Poetry Review, Montaigne at Piggly Wiggly
Southern Poetry Review, Now Playing
The Dark Horse, Losing One's Hats
The Georgia Review, Father's Day: Looking West
Poetry Porch, Saturday Afternoon Music, Portrait of an Old Man,
        by Memling
The Southwest Review, Ash Wednesday: Coffee at Starbucks
Able Muse, Waiting for the Angel
Sewanee Theological Review, Café du Monde
Painted Bride Quarterly, Bach, Onomatopoeia, and the Wreck, Apprenticing
        Your Ghost
Think Journal, A Garden Much Like Thought Itself
Innisfree Poetry Journal, A Creature from the Murk
The Cumberland Review, A Connoisseur of Wind

Publisher: Leah Huete de Maines
Editor: Christen Kincaid
Author Photo: Robert Butler
Cover Design: Elizabeth Maines McCleavy

Order online: www.finishinglinepress.com
also available on amazon.com

Author inquiries and mail orders:
Finishing Line Press
PO Box 1626
Georgetown, Kentucky 40324
USA

Contents

To an Unknown Confidant

So if, like me, you often think—lets say,
while folding laundry, sorting forks and spoons,
or staring at your pile of unread books—
about some famous bridge, of ending it,
one melancholy night, with one last leap
into the river's mystery, but then—
remembering the long-awaited, still
unwritten chapter of your stalled life story
in which your deeper narrative, the slow
momentum of your famous meant-to-be,
is fabulously revealed—decide you won't,
and if, like me—sick of the bridge routine—
you want to talk until we sort things out,
dinner's on me. You won't believe the wine!

Kleos, or Fame

*The rank and file I shall not name; I could not
if I were gifted with ten tongues and voices . . .*
The Iliad, Book 2, trans. by R. Fitzgerald

I'm doing thirty in the caution zone,
and feeling sorry for myself I'm not
somebody famous Homer might have named—
until a cop steps out, holds up his hand,
and frowns, as I snap to, quick hit the brake,
and spare the school-free kids crossing the street.

Two teen tots in the lead look pretty smart:
her high-top sneakers match her backpack, pink;
he wears his Falcons' cap brim backward, cool.
A dozen more, in multicolored gear,
step forth in fluent order, two by two,
buoyant and noisy in elastic shoes,

eager to break into the keep of those
who wait for them beneath September's trees,
eager to talk about their day, the cool,
the fun, the boring things they had to do,
eager to hug the ones who take their hands
and guide them home. And so, I get it now:

this is a moment in a gentle war
against whatever odds diminish hope,
waged by the ones I cannot name, the rank
and file who teach, who sweep the halls, who keep
the peace, who plant petunias in the urns
beside the schoolhouse door. They have to, yes;

work seems to be a thing we have to do.
And yet I think they keep on showing up
because they're stubborn, in the right way, brave,
and choose, deep down, to stick it to despair,
determined, generations down the line,
to take back history from violence.

Montaigne at Piggly Wiggly

> *"Branler," to totter, shake, or move inconstantly.*
> *A Dictionarie of the French and English Tongues,*
> *by Randle Cotgrave*

"Tout branle," I think, remembering Montaigne,
watching the clouds evolve and race a cold,
midwinter moon above the parking lot
at Piggly Wiggly, Monteagle, Tennessee.
"Tout branle," I warn the few, remaining cars,
steeled in their various states of disrepair:
we live uncertainly on shaky ground.

The sign—its "l" and "y" unlit—reads "Pigg."
And there the happy fellow is: Himself,
in neon pink, grinning with just a hint
of mockery, as if deep down he knows,
ce cochon philosophe, that at the core
of who we are, we discombobulate,
and disappear into a nameless dark.

But now another memory comes to mind:
it's summer in Ohio. Dad is treating us
to nickel day at *Euclid Beach*. We've got—
speaking of ontological upheaval—
a dollar each to spend, that's twenty rides:
bumpity-bump, and loop the loop, and down
into the scary tunnel, out again.

On either side the entrance to the fun,
stand ten foot tall, hill-billy Pa and Ma,
mechanical but smart, laughing as if
they'll split their innards at the sight of us,
eagerly waiting, ticket in hand, to soar
and plummet, roll, and hurtle upside down,
lurching and screaming toward the final hill.

And so—by way of several continents,
no other destiny than this: then this,
then this—the curves and slides and bumps have brought
me here: a Piggly Wiggly parking lot
in Tennessee. Okay! I have a list
my wife made out of all the things we need.
The liquor store near-by has got good wine.

And now, for just a moment, I slow down.
The clouds are gone, and up above, the moon—
a silent, grinning, cold midwinter moon—
looks down at me, alone among the cars.
I stand, awed for a moment by the strange,
the empty, moonlit stillness of this place,
then laugh, quite happily, at being here.

Now Playing

With thanks to Joseph Kesselring

You're ten years old, and living in Ohio,
your house above the river, on the heights.
It's summer, almost dusk. In your back yard,
with your invisible but magic sword,
you're fending off imaginary monsters,
when all at once there's music—a carousel?
a carnival?—filling the evening air.
You race around the house to see what's what,
and way down there, rounding the river bend,
is an old-fashioned boat, a wedding cake
with paddle wheels, lit with a thousand bulbs,
a floating theater, you later learn,
about to dock, sell tickets, play the play,
and Saturday—guess what?—you get to go.

It's all about this crazy family,
two loony aunts, their nephew, Mortimer,
a wandering corpse, two weirdo brothers,
and lots of bodies buried in the basement.
But in the end, the hero, Mortimer—
who saves the day and could be you—
gets beautiful Elaine—who could be Mimi,
your grade school crush—and off they go to start
their honeymoon. And Sunday, as you watch
the boat, full steam ahead, calliope
full blast, vanish around the bend, what if—
you can't help wonder—Mimi and you were both
on board, and starring in that crazy play?
This happened more than sixty years ago.

Somewhere in Tennessee

It's late for coffee, but I need a boost,
still a long way from home. Not many here.
A single woman, Edward-Hopper-type,
like me, alone and in a corner. The staff—
a tall, smart-looking, he's-in-charge-here guy,
his lady-buddy, modest, plump, and fun—
find things to wipe and polish, put away,
and laugh about.
                And lounging center stage,
a study gig from time to time lets out
a caffeinated whoop, a genial bunch
of college kids with well-marked, five-pound books.
Biology, it seems, is where it's at,
the now-we-get-it science of the laws
that secretly condition us, while we
sit perking up our brains with something strong.

Speaking of brains on high, what's this I feel?
A sudden, deep-felt surge of sympathy
for my new java kin. Biology
of coffee can't explain, I want to think,
what's happening deep in me now, an urge
to send these strangers telepathically
power to cope with what's up day to day
with such finesse, when they have kids, the kids
know how to carry on the dream.
                                I need
to go, but stay here, try and memorize
these souls on high in magic Tennessee,
giggling and working, solving mysteries,
or in a corner smiling to herself.
I know they'll leave here ready to begin.
I get one for the road, three bags of beans.

Whoopee! Another 'Carpe Diem' Poem

"Thank you," the flight boss lady says, with more
than usual zeal, as my squashed coffee cup,
tossed in a graceful, hyperbolic arc,
plops in her outstretched plastic bag. She nods
her head and balances her way in heels
deftly along a somewhat tipsy aisle,
as I take up my book, a heavy one
I'm counting on—being a theorist,
of sorts—to help me fortify my yet
evolving theory of the whole. But wait!
What was that cup maneuver all about?
I need to play it over in my head.

We're on a bumpy Nashville-New York flight;
the one in charge, in really risky heels,
finding her balance with an agile grace,
rounds up the coffee clutter. Smart guy—me—
squeezing his portion of the plastic mess
into a rough, compact projectile, arcs
the missile with a perfect, smart-guy aim
into the bulging, yawning sack. "Whoopee,"
she nods her head, and I nod back, "Damn right!"
And we both laugh! Enthusiastically!
So I put down my book, and she moves on.
Time for a theory of the well-lived now!

Hyperbole! A little excess! Fun!
'Now' as a chance to fiddle with the moment,
knowing the moment is in flight, and could,
at any moment, spin into a dive,
thanks to systemic flaw, or human fault,
or cosmic whim. So yes to hyper-heels,
a whoopee trick, spontaneous huzzah,
complicity between two strangers, each
going another way to unknown ends,
but coping with the moment with pizzazz.
And that's my little theory, crumpled up,
and hyper-flung in your direction. Catch!

Losing One's Hats

The one you think about the most was blue.
You loved that hat, pliant and soft, and yet
it held its shape, the crown perfectly round
and subtly oversized, the stitching tight,
assertive, and the brim a little floppy.
It was a perfect hat, a bit too much,
that made you want to say, I am alive,
and wearing blue.
                    You lost it in the wind
at Forty-Sixth and Broadway, going North;
a sudden gust came at you from behind,
and good-bye hat. It blew into the air,
and soaring like a Frisbee over Broadway,
dropped into traffic on the other side
and disappeared, for good, under a truck,
totally vanished. Gone forever. Damn!

So who, or what's to blame? A butterfly
in Argentina? Cosmic Justice? You?
The Greeks were smart. The Greeks did not wear hats,
except in war. They knew: to walk around,
wearing a hat, proclaiming to the gods,
I am alive and wearing blue, or pink,
or green, or purple, not a good idea,
hubris; Zeus in his wrath would strike you flat.

Wang Wei, the poet, on the other hand,
would not have been perturbed, drinking all night,
beside a lake, and dancing with the fish
beneath the moon, or just letting his mind
float with the morning mist among the pines;
he understood the Tao, and its ways.

And you do too, when you're a little drunk,
as you are now, and ready to forgive the gods,
and tell how beautiful the moment was,
in retrospect, when the great Tao blew
your hat away in a great soaring arc,
perfect hyperbole into the all,
and left you with the impulse to find words
to celebrate your hat and its demise,
and shout, I am alive, not feeling blue.

Father's Day: Looking West

"Is man no more than this?" King Lear

From twelve floors up, looking across the roofs,
we get a glimpse of Jersey, glimpse of Hudson,
evening sky. Window wide open. Breeze.
My folks—my mother's ninety-three and blind,
my father's ninety-five and crippled—sit
by the window, eating quietly. Below,
there is a tiny park, with benches, trees,
places to hide and seek, jump rope.
From time to time, a block away on Broadway,
the number one train—elevated here—
rattles along toward Harlem and the Heights.
The neighborhood is pleasantly supplied:
boutiques with produce lavishly displayed,
a bakery, a liquor store with decent French.
So life's okay.
              In here, it's winding down.
And as I hand my parents food, or try
to tell them once again what day it is,
or when their next appointments are, or why—
for the hundredth time—they shouldn't feel depressed,
I can't help wondering just what this life
is meant to be about.
              It's Father's Day.
I bring the cake, uncork the special bottle,
and so we sit and have dessert. From time
to time, my mother takes my hand. "It is
so comforting," she says, "to have you here."

I pour some more Vouvray. My father wipes
the butter cream from his glazed lips, and lifts
his glass, and sips. My mother talks of books
she wants to read when she gets back her sight.
I don't say anything. I pour more wine.
And all at once, my father, still a priest,
sings out, full voice, snatches of evensong,

"Lord, open thou our lips, and let our mouths
show forth thy praise." And then sits quietly.
We hear the sounds of children's games outside.
It's almost dusk. The subway rumbles North.

Saturday Afternoon Music

The Balcony Cafe: NY's Metropolitan Museum

"Scatter my ashes now," he softly shouts,
sipping, and listening to Rachmaninoff,
a suite for two extremely grand pianos,
and four extravagantly brilliant hands,

his gesture, too, extravagant, as he,
in solitary celebration, sits,
feeling his residue of soul release
in loose, exhilarate arpeggios,

a prelude, surely, to the ultimate—
these notes, these secret possibilities
of wood and steel, so deftly hammered out
by fingers fluent as the speed of thought—

the latent oscillations of the self,
loosed into being in the heavenly air.

Ash Wednesday: Coffee at Starbucks

I

"By lot India fell to Judas Thomas, also called Didymus.
And he did not wish to go, saying that he was not able to
go on account of the weakness of his body."
The Acts of Thomas

"May God be in my head and in my understanding."
Old Sarum Primer

Nua, I did forget, and here I sit,
comfy and snug in Starbuck's, Mid-town West,
sipping the beverage of the Demiurge,
and browsing through a stack of brand new books:
Gnostic Discoveries, Beyond Belief,
The Secret Revelation of Saint John.
And in the Gospel of the Doubting One,
I read: "Know what is there in front of you;
then what you cannot see will be revealed."

I start to look around at what is there,
my nerve cells humming quietly, Hurrah,
for coffee and the arch-creator fiend
who tends the furnace at the heart of things,
who makes caffeine, excites the blood, the buzz
of business and talk, laughter, the hiss
of steam, and Coltrane on the speakers—cool.

Outside, the darkening streets are full of purpose:
the lights go on, the traffic hits the gas,
and everybody on the sidewalk moves,
even the ones the Demiurge mucked up,
the paraplegic pushing at his wheels,
the schizophrenic shrinking through the crowd,
and all who hate their bodies and their lives.

I open up the Times, and there, page one:
a pregnant woman, disemboweled, dead,
lies in the desert of Darfur, her face
smothered in flies.

May God be in my head.

II

It's tricky curving to Mbale, down
these fifteen miles of slippery, washed out road.
We're in the Ford, souped-up and custom-tough
for Africa. It's fifty years ago.
You sit beside me, Nua, shake your head.
"Fever," you say, and then just sit. In back,
the mother from the village rocks and hums,
her baby quiet, shivering in her arms.
We reach the clinic, join the sick who wait,
patient with hope, huddled beneath the trees.
"Fever," the medical assistant says,
and shakes his head. He turns to someone else.
The baby's lips are white, the body limp.

By miracle, it seems, the news has spread.
As we drive home, a hundred women stand
along the road. They stand there quietly,
and watch us pass. More women come. Then more.
Their daughters come. The mother starts to wail,
with her whole being rocks, and sobs, finds sound,
or so it seems, for the whole, grieving earth.
And all along the road, the women stand,
and watch the body home.

III

Before I left,
one night, we sat around, drank beer, and talked;
and then there was a quiet moment. "Promise,

you won't forget us, David?" "Don't be silly."
"Promise?"
           I don't remember who wrote last.
I loved to come to dinner at your house:
steamed plantains, rice, and peanut sauce; if God
were generous a chicken, cooked in broth
with beans and maize, and curry from the shop.
At noon, out back, your mother built the fire,
pounded the peanuts in the pestle. At two,
she put the plantains on to cook. The sun,
as always in eternal summer, set
at six. A single gas lamp hung above
the table, lit our faces in the dark.
Your sister knelt in turn before each guest,
held out warm water in a bowl, and soap.
We washed our hands. Your father gave the thanks.

So I do think of you from time to time,
and wonder what became of you, if this
is how it was: you and your family
at table, during the presidential scourge,
then suddenly alert as the truck braked
out front, and rifle buts broke down the door.
Or maybe you survived, are teaching school,
or maybe, like your father, you are now
a priest.
           Forgive me, Nua; when the plane
touched down at Idlewild, I felt the bump
go through me like a shout, O God, I'm here!
And in the taxi, headed for the world—
the windows down, the radio tuned loud
to rock and roll, and all my souvenirs
beside me in a bag: a monkey skin,
an ivory handled knife, a carved giraffe,
a mask, a hookah and a kudu horn—
forgive me, Nua, I forgot.

IV

                              It's night
outside. In here, I close my eyes, tune in
to Mingus, jabber, clatter, exchange of cash,
musique concrète, the murmur of what is,
where I float now, suspended, listening,
a lucky one, who needs sometimes to speak
a kind of praise for things: book, table, cup,
street, window, crowd, the evidence of what?
The demon-architect? The genius
of viruses, the drummer of the dance,
the many-figured one, the demiurge?
Or something far more deeply interfused?

I fold the Times, and stow my books, and join
the energy of night, the dinner crowd,
the movie crowd, the hubbub of the bars.
The theaters are lit, and cabs are hard
to get. I'm meeting friends at six. And here
and there, I pass a penitent, the place
of intuition dabbed with ash. Nua,
I did forget.
                    May God be in my head.

Portrait of an Old Man, by Memling

European Galleries, New York's Metropolitan

I come here often, stand here wondering
just what this old man knows, his face
revealed against a night of background dark,
and brought to presence in an amber glow,
the source—his secret knowledge?—mysterious,
hands also lit, clasped softly in repose.

Or maybe he's forgotten what he knew,
his knowledge music now, enlightenment,
gently unraveling his neural snarls
and loosening the corners of his lips.
Although the paint is thickly cracked, he's there,
about to smile; his music brings him through.

A gift! If we wait quietly with him,
we may begin to hear the music too.

Waiting for the Angel

"What do you make of this?" my mother asks,
then lies back down. Her bed's the couch. She's blind,
and ninety-five. Today, August nineteenth,
my father's ninety-eight. He's having wine,
but he's too weak to sip it through a straw,
and so I feed it to him with a spoon.
We've brought his bed, mechanical, equipped
with safety bars into the living room,
close to my mother. "What do you make of this,"
she asks again and lies back down. She knows,
unconsciously, something is not quite right:
my father's dying, helpless, incontinent,
his six-two frame twisted and shrunk, skin loose,
discolored, bruised. "It's time to go," he says.
I put my ear close to his lips. "What, dad?"
"Lets go." "Go where?" He tries to move his legs,
"Go where?" "Back home." "But Dad, this is our home."
He looks at me, confused, tries to sit up,
but can't. "What is he saying?" mother asks.
"Don't worry, mom. Dad's just a bit confused."
"I don't know what to make of this," she says.
I put on mother's favorite, "On Wings
of Song," with Jimmy Galway playing flute.

Things start to settle down. I fill my glass,
and sit beside the window, twelve floors up,
looking toward Jersey in the dark. It's cool
for August. People are heading out. "Let's go,"
a voice calls in my head. And yes, it would
be nice to be out there among the quick,
catching the breeze in some café down Broadway.

Instead, I pour more wine, and lolling in
my chair, not knowing what to make of this,
surrender to the world: my parent's breath,
the laughter in the street, the August air,

and Jimmy Galway's flute, our lullaby,
Wesendonk Leider, number 1. "Let go,"
the music says, "an angel will float down,
and gently lift the soul gen *Himmel hebt.*"
The wine within me shouts, "Let it be so."

Café du Monde

It's not the Armagnac, although the wind
seems more to him than just the wind, now,
beneath the trees on upper Broadway, June,
Café du Monde. Astonishing,
the air, this evening, this gentleness,
this promise of some blessing yet to be,
the sound of nothing blowing through the leaves,
the sound of nothing to be done but heal
and listen to the murmur of the world,
the festive bustle in the gathering dark
becoming nothing, now, for years and years
to come. Now quietly the listener,
inebriate, lifts up his glass, salutes,
in gratitude, the late, enduring light.

On Buying Time

"Then I defy you, stars."
Shakespeare, The Passionate Pilgrim

I needed soap, the usual, whatever.
But standing in the store, I thought again:
I'm older now; I need to do research.
And so I took a moment, read the fine print,
assessed the fabulous ingredients
of fifteen brands of soap, and chose the one
that boasts, "this subtly crafted soap defies
the deleterious effects of time."
I bought five bars, now lather lavishly,
check in the mirror more than once a day,
hoping to catch the miracle effects
of aloe-vera, cocoa-butter, hemp,
and mint, but not just ordinary mint,
an ancient Aztec mint from Mexico.

It was that word "defy" persuaded me,
a sturdy word, defy, Shakespearean.
It helps me go defiantly about,
smelling of Aztec mint, ignoring time.
Bravado? Sure. At any moment now,
some leakage in the cranium or gut,
some blockage in the lungs, some fractious glitch
will call my bluff and dump defiance down
a deep, deep hole. So here's the strategy:
more pharmacopeia, more witchery,
more running to the store to buy more stuff:
essence of this, tincture of that, cod's brain,
shark's bone, venom of sea anemone.
Put magic in a bottle and I'll buy it.

Learning to Cope: That Big Store on the Mall

"Nature herself especially rejoices in variety,"
Desiderius Erasmus, On Copia of Words and Ideas (1513)

Just look at this, Erasmus! Copia!
The whole wide-world caboodle priced to sell,
from rabbit food to cross bows for the kill!
There's paint in tints to tempt the subtlest whim:
Pink Organdy, Mint Julep, Harvest Moon;
widgets to miter, chisel, chop, or gouge,
and all you need to nurse a rose, or clip
a bush, or gut a trout, or trap a mole,
to poison bugs, or barbecue God's creatures.

I'm on a roll, Erasmus, I admit,
browsing around, mouthing the snazzy names
of high-speed shoes and mumbo-jumbo pills,
of triple-whammy candy bars and snacks,
of hyper-tonic drinks, hyperbole
and onomatopoeia everywhere.
I'm in the mood, imagining new brands
out loud: Bazooka Aspirin, Ding-Dong Gum,
lots more. Now I'm a poet of the aisles!

I'm sure as hell at sea. There's so much stuff,
I can't remember what I came to get.
It's time to get a decent lunch. But look,
Erasmus! Piles of Holland bulbs on sale!
Now I know why I'm here! I need ten bags,
the super size, ten different kinds. I'll plant
until the ground turns hard. March, April, May,
Nature herself will urge us to rejoice:
a copious variety of blooms.

Bach, Onomatopoeia, and the Wreck

For all we knew, it was a random chunk
of interstellar rock, the rear-end crash
that brought us to a halt. Dinner was out,
of course, and the Bach too, I realized,
feeling it in my neck, and standing there
in the rain, examining my totaled car,
the guilty driver soaked, in tears. The cops
were nice enough, did what they had to do
efficiently. The wrecker did show up,
eventually, and we began to cope.
And since it's now collision story time,
the word I'm hearing in my head is 'thud'.

There's 'clunk', of course, or 'jolt', 'wham-bang', or 'thwack'.
'Thwack' has that sudden, can't-be-happening feel,
as in, "I was just sitting, reading Kant,
when suddenly, inside my head, I felt
this 'thwack', and everything went blank." But no!
The word that bangs the scary drum is 'thud',
essence—onomatopoetically—
of impact, 'thud', from dice, to hand-grenade,
to asteroid. I need the stupid 'd'
of 'doo-doo', 'dodo', 'dude', or 'dud', or 'dead'.
'You're-done-for-d" is what we're up against;
you never know when out of nowhere, 'thud'!

But on the other hand, there's Bach: the Bach
we missed, the works for cello solo. Bach:
initial 'b', a kind of plosive bump,
terminal 'ch', a bit of friction in
the throat, but in between the 'b' and 'ch',
the 'ah', release: sustained and open, 'ah'.
Think of the bow colliding with the string,
a subtle thud, a scrape, and out floats Bach,
genial Bach-analia of dark
and light, a theory of the universe
as music: bang, and then the sarabande,
the minuet, the allemande, the gigue.

Maybe I'm Talking to You

Hello, discouraged ones, you fed-up cooks,
done-with-it-now-for-ever gardeners,
despondent poets, artists of daily life,
it's me, your talky, self-appointed uncle,
who's sounding off from somewhere in your head.

You lost your trowel planting hollyhocks,
put too much sugar in the wedding cake,
tore up your draft of Ode in Praise of Praise,
and everywhere you look, neglected gizmos,
scorched utensils, more pencils than you need.

To make things worse, you listen to the news,
somehow associate your daily mess—
perfecting what your heart prompts you to do—
with history, that other, bloody mess.
You can't help wondering, "what's the use?"

Okay, let's talk about your silly cake,
essential to essential celebration,
your hollyhocks, a dozen shades of pink
that mark our way along the garden path,
poems in praise of morning, noon, and night.

What if you're on the side of those who hope,
who strive to stanch the flow of blood, the will
to power, suffering, who work to clear
the wreckage, drown—at least for now—the fires,
our misbegotten, catastrophic fires?

Maybe they're hoping too—remembering cake,
and hollyhocks, and poems—that history
may yet become the art of day to day.

Apprenticing Your Ghost

Some Friday night, it might be worth a try:
after a glass or two of French, a page
or more of some ambitious book,
let go into the couch. When you wake up,
lights on, at 3 am, not sure just where,
or who you are, assume you've died, a ghost,
for the first time, returning to your house.
In your confusion, look around, and breathe
the aether of this place. You lived here once,
or sort of, passing through, hopped up to win
and knock the bastards for a loop. But now
you're dead and there's no rush. So give the couch
a bounce or two, discovering again
how cunningly it's made for reading, naps,
and listening to Bach. And say it, "couch",
with the full vigor of your new-found voice.
Stand up, letting your feet sink in the rug,
and say it, "rug". There's the whole room to go,
"piano", "roses", "coffee table", "mug",
your voice becoming stronger, almost as if
you were alive, almost as if you loved
these things, needed to greet them all by name.
Now what about your missing ones, the ones
who used to live upstairs, or out of state?
Call out to them. Maybe you'll wake them too.

A Garden Much like Thought Itself

This pathway through the garden he has made
is a long sentence, turning in, and in,
with no beginning, no determined end,
finding its syntax as it goes, around
a stand of Budleia, plotted to lure
the lovely Lepidoptera and bees;
in ovals underneath the oaks and birds
to see the pink Astilbe and the ferns,
the Coral Bells, the Lamium in bloom,
then on to check the roses in the sun
with all their pretty names, and back around,
and in and out again, until the seeker stands
amazed beyond the sense of anything
but where he is, then goes around again,
and speaks the word for everything he sees.

In Magic Tennessee

At fifty miles an hour, you're driving home,
on impulse check the sacred finger. Bare!
No wedding band! Did you forget today
to put it on, at random set it down,
your sixty years of marriage, pure gold ring?
You hit the gas, say nothing to your wife,
head for your room, open the sacred box,
the tiny, jeweled box. No! nothing there!

You check the kitchen counter, bathroom sink,
library table, front seat of the car,
wherever, desperately, you think to look.
Drive back to Piggly Wiggly? CVS?
Or what if there's a jeweler in Monteagle?
The Amish Hippie? Google's only hint.
The sympathetic lady shakes her head,
her hand dismissing all the costume junk.

"Your best bet's Tullahoma," says the lady.
Okay. But you don't want to leave your wife,
—dependent on your care—alone that long,
and you remember, driving home, the mulch,
ten bags of pine bark mulch, pulled from the trunk
before you left this morning to run errands,
piled in the driveway, near the garden's edge.
Maybe it slipped off then. You hit the gas.

No luck. You pick the bags up one by one,
check underneath, and all around.
Nothing but gravel, dirt, and pine bark mulch.
Disconsolate, you stand there, wondering.
Maybe it's time for Tullahoma. Wait!
Is that? There, in the sunlit gravel, gold!
In gratitude, you reach down, gently grip
the magic ring. It's time to fix her lunch.

A Creature from the Murk

It could have been a boneless baby seal,
the lump of life you rescued from the murk
of the pond's deep. You came there in a dream,
on impulse waded through the ooze, and eased
your hands into the verdant mystery,
then deep into the muck of bottom leaves,
and pulled her out, a glob of furry life.
You looked into her tiny opal eyes,
and felt her breathing in your palms, you made
a goo-goo sound, on impulse hugged her softly
against your chest until the dream moved on.
But you remembered her when you woke up,
and think of her sometimes, especially when
the usual checks and contradictions tempt
you toward solution with a gun. You hug
the memory of that life, and you move on.

One Day It Has to Be

To an unknown soprano,
Sewanee Summer Music Festival, 2021

One day she'll sing the magic note,
and history opt out, violence ease,
gentle vibration tune our will to be.

She may not know it but she will;
we felt it through and through that afternoon:
something astonishing is on the verge.

Magic will guide her to its secret space;
she'll work her octaves, conjuring her power,
her magical associate on cello.

And now she's ready, magic word has spread,
musicians seated, orchestra in tune,
mysteriously alert. The hall is packed.

Not there? Imagine all that's happening:
she hums some notes, the cello complicates,
the smart ones catch on quickly, off they go,

invent the weather of the aria:
accelerando breeze, *festoso* storm.
Too late to stop her now. She's on the loose.

The hall erupts, and history bows out,
the celebration spills into the street.
The universal tour will soon begin.

A Connoisseur of Wind

He knows we cannot trust the wind, and yet,
"Listen," he says, and so we do, and wait,
patiently, underneath the frozen trees.
But hearing nothing in the wind but wind,
we start to leave. He shakes a finger, no,
and smiles, and so—hoping to catch a hint
of what it is he thinks he hears in all
this steady innuendo of the end—
we wait some more. But listening for what?
More windy variations on a theme
of nothing? A whispered rumor of what is?
We watch him, as he smiles, eyes closed,
swaying in rhythm with the ebb and swell,
then looks at us, and bows, and leaves us here.

David Landon is the Bishop Juhan Professor of Theatre Emeritus at the University of the South in Sewanee. He won the American Academy Poetry Prize as an undergraduate at Harvard, where he was class poet. More recent poems have appeared in *Able Muse* (Write Prize), *Southwest Review* (Marr Prize, runner-up), *Georgia Review* (Lorraine Williams Prize, featured finalist), and elsewhere. As an actor he has performed with the Nashville, Alabama, and New York Shakespeare Festivals, with the Provincetown and New Orleans Tennessee Williams' Festivals. Several of his undergraduate poems were republished in the *Harvard Advocate Centennial Anthology* (T. S. Eliot, Wallace Stevens, E.E. Cummings, etc.).

www.ingramcontent.com/pod-product-compliance
Lightning Source LLC
Chambersburg PA
CBHW022057080426
42734CB00009B/1384